PIANO VOCAL GUITAR

BEST OF k.d. lang

Cover photo © Jeri Heiden

ISBN 978-1-4234-3482-5

HAL•LEONARD®
CORPORATION

7777 W. BLUEMOUND RD. P.O. BOX 13819 MILWAUKEE, WI 53213

Visit Hal Leonard Online at
www.halleonard.com

BIG BONED GAL

Words and Music by k.d. lang
and BEN MINK

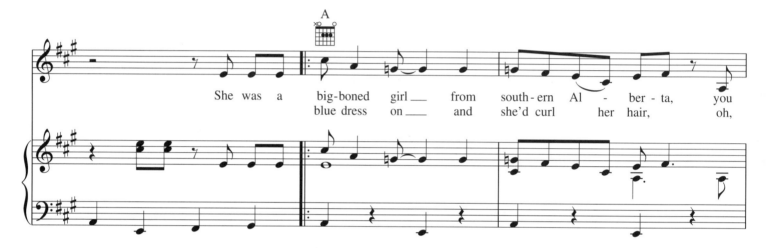

She was a big-boned girl ___ from south-ern Al-ber-ta, you
blue dress on ___ and she'd curl her hair, oh,

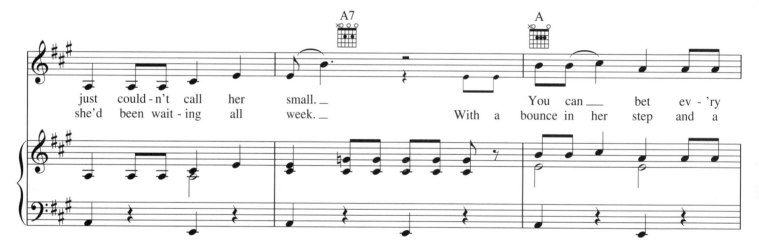

just could-n't call her small. ___ You can ___ bet ev-'ry
she'd been wait-ing all week. ___ With a bounce in her step and a

Sa-tur-day night she'd be head-ed for the le-gion hall. Put her
wig-gle in her walk, she'd be swing-ing down the

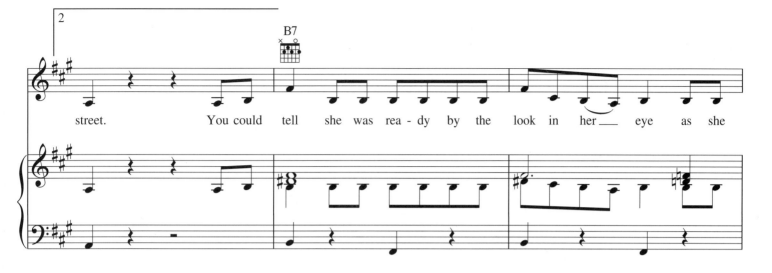

street. You could tell she was rea- dy by the look in her ___ eye as she

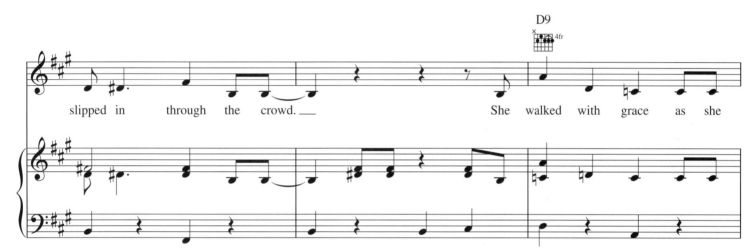

slipped in through the crowd. ___ She walked with grace as she

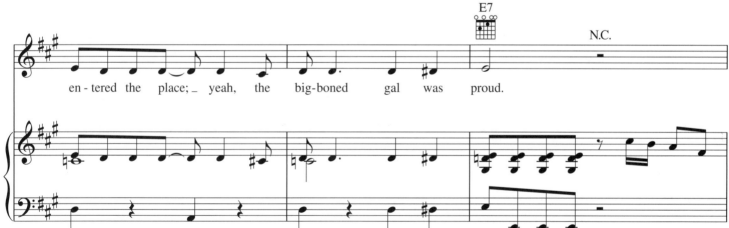

en- tered the place; _ yeah, the big-boned gal was proud.

Now

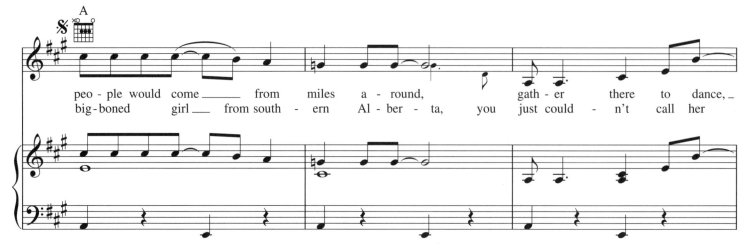

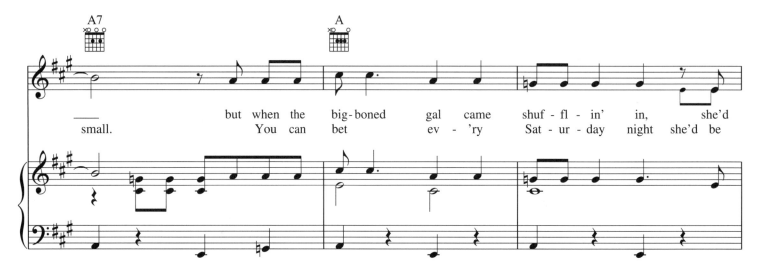

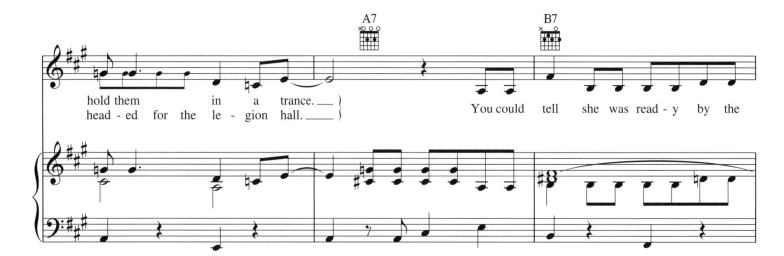

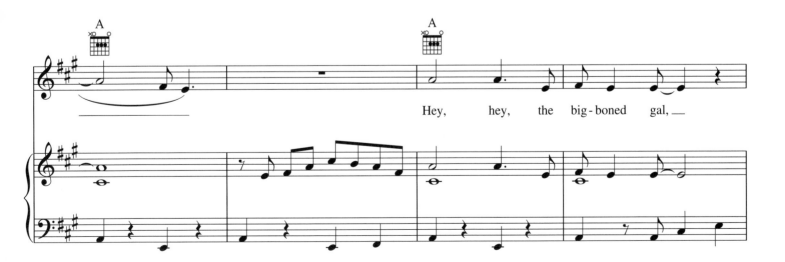

ain't no doubt__ she's a nat - u - ral,___ reel - in' and a - rock - in' and she's

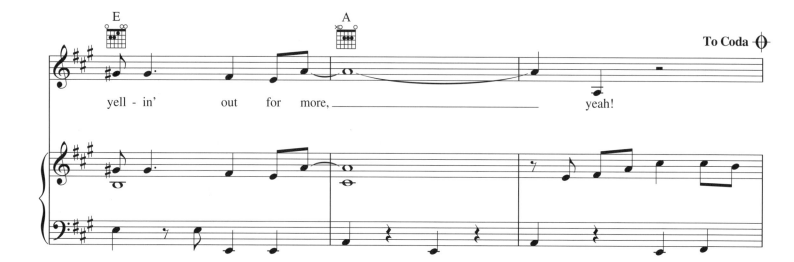

yell - in' out for more, _____ yeah!

To Coda ⊕

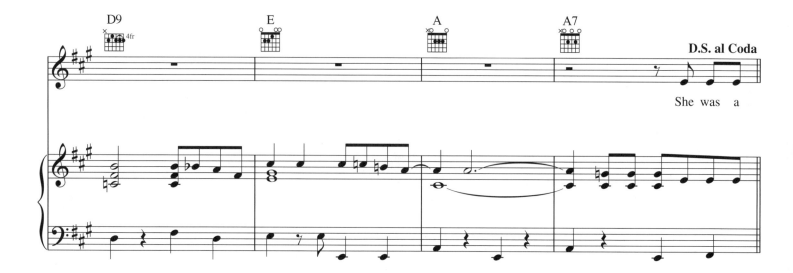

D.S. al Coda

She was a

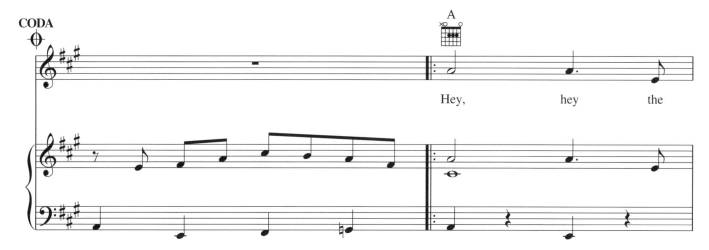

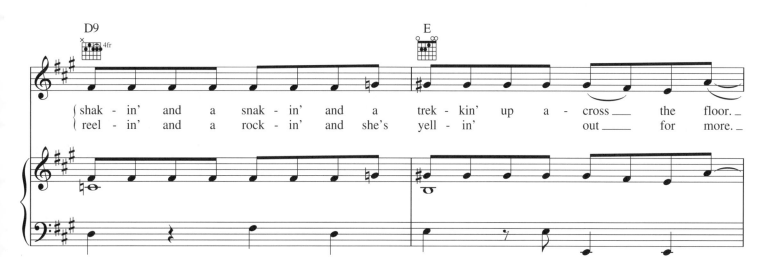

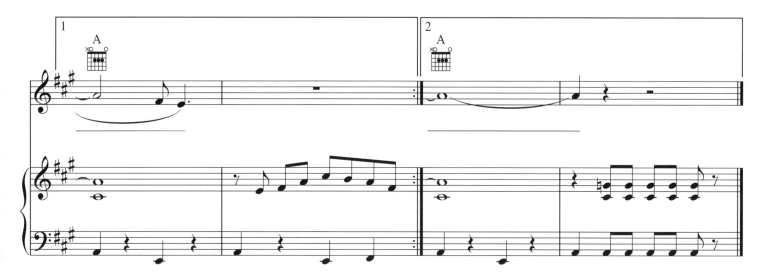

CONSTANT CRAVING

Words and Music by k.d. lang
and BEN MINK

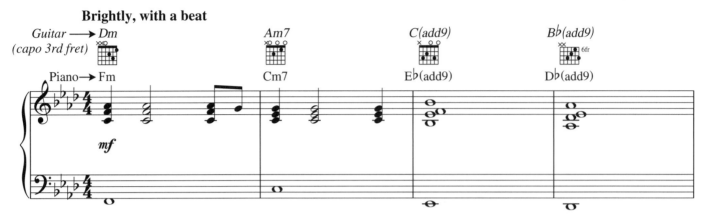

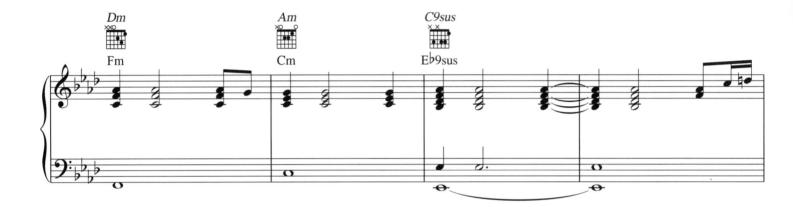

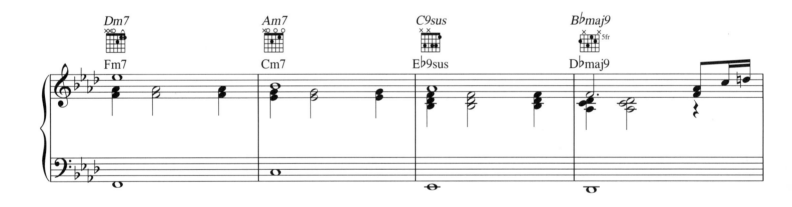

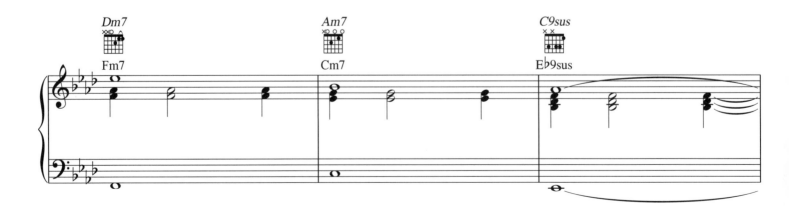

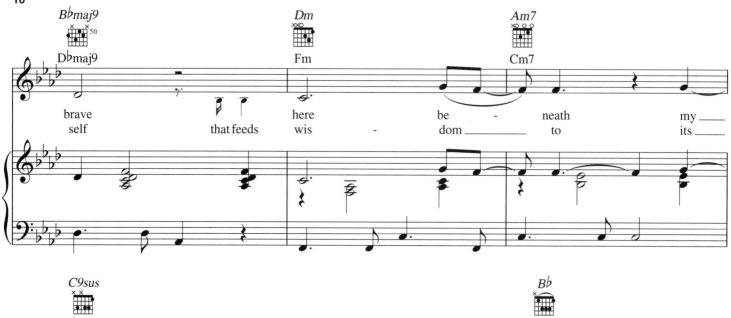

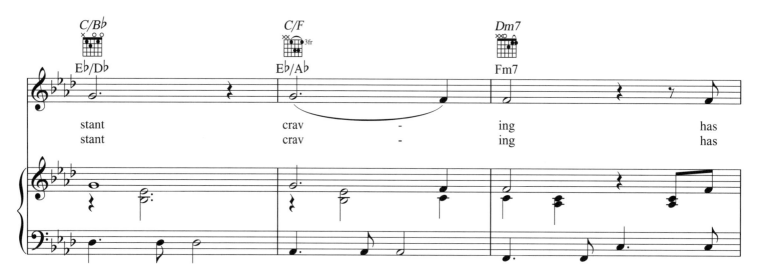

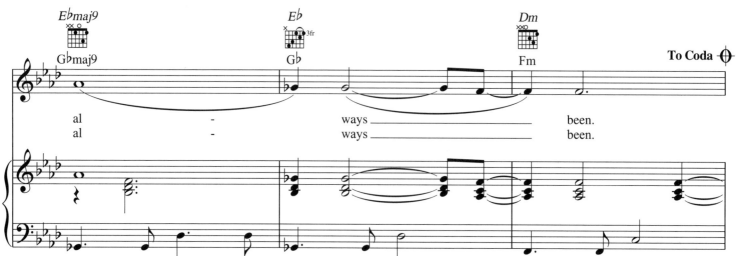

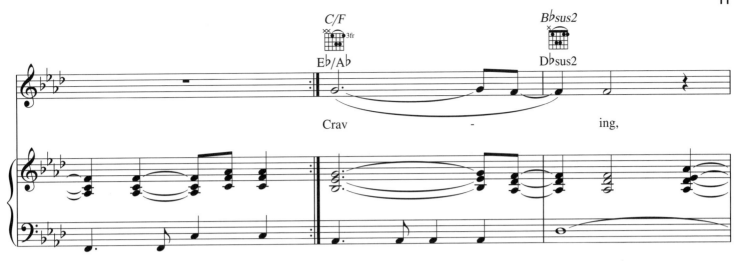

al - ways ___ been.

D.S. al Coda

CODA

Con -

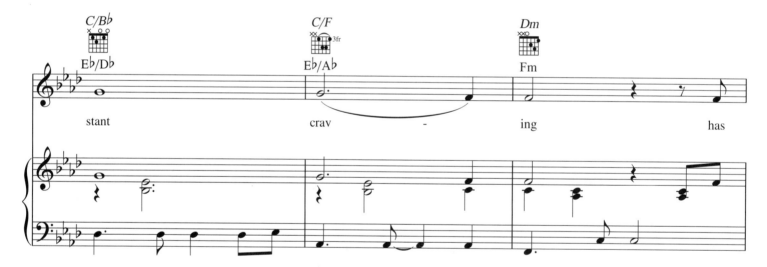

stant crav - ing has

al - ways been.

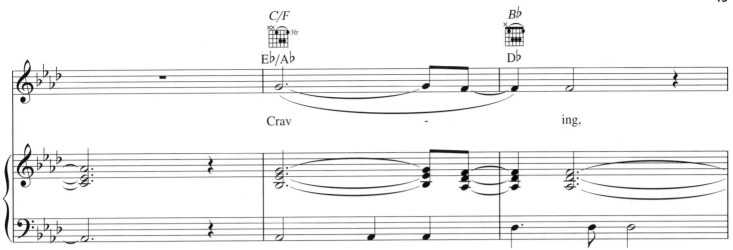

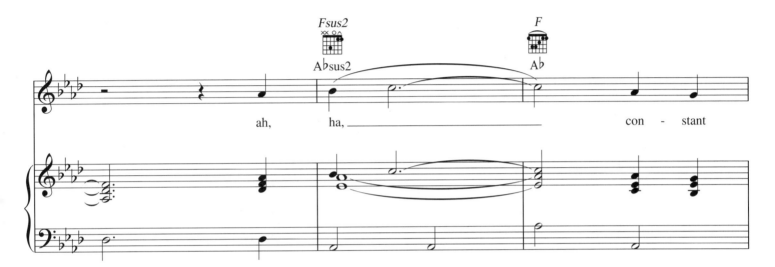

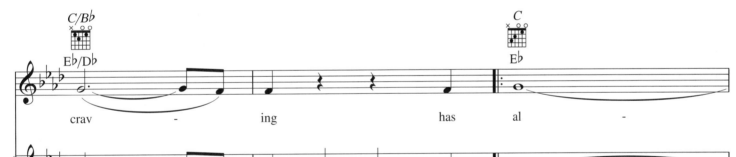

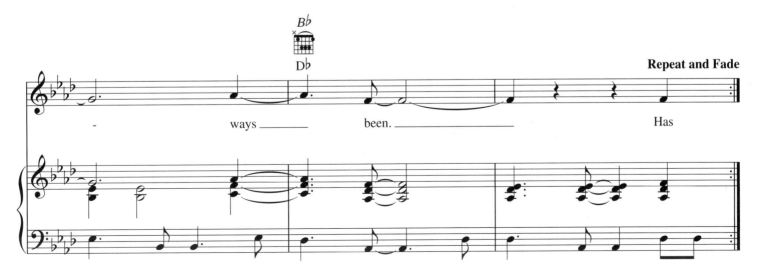

EXTRAORDINARY THING

Words and Music by k.d. lang
and ABE LABORIEL

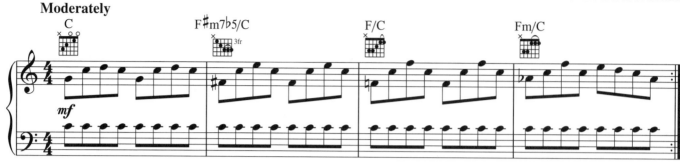

My or - di - nar - y days ____ are spent ____

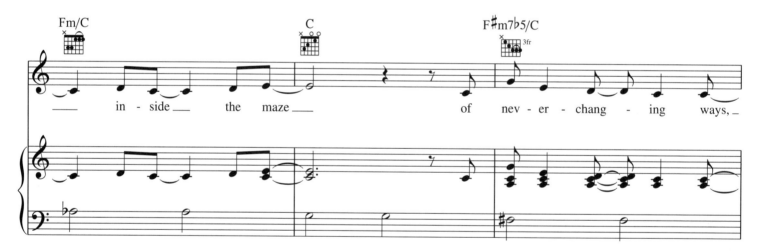

____ in - side ____ the maze ____ of nev - er - chang - ing ways, ____

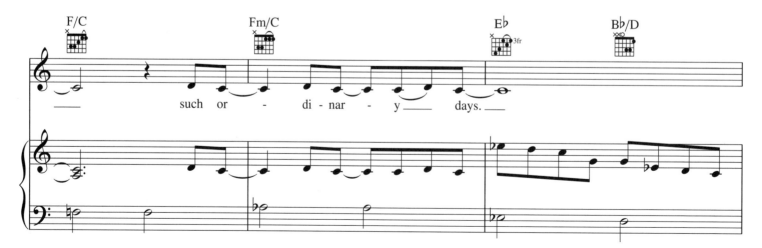

____ such or - di - nar - y ____ days. ____

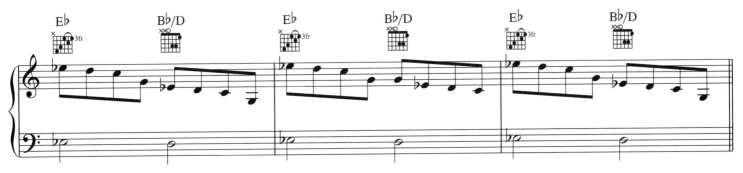

And my or - di - nar - y ___ spin ___
My or - di - nar - y ___ game, ___ pre -

showed it - self ___ a - gain. _____
dict - a - ble ___ and plain, _____

It nev - er seemed ___ to end, ___
has nev - er been ___ the same ___

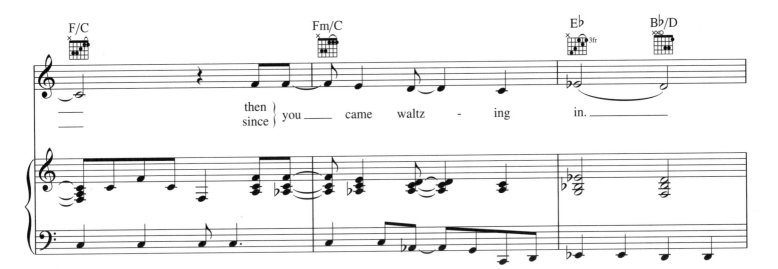

___ then } you ___ came waltz - ing in. _____
___ since }

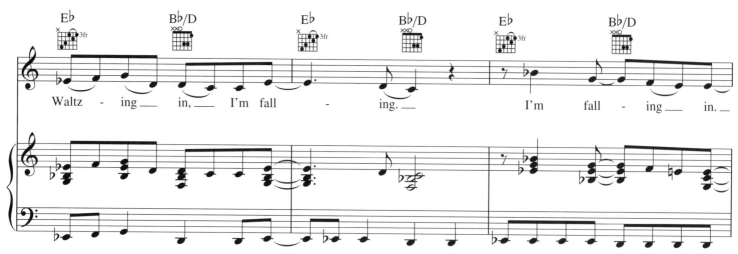

Waltz - ing __ in, __ I'm fall - ing. __ I'm fall - ing __ in. __

__ I nev - er knew __ the likes __ of you, __ ex - traor -

- di - nar - y __ thing. __ I do __ be - lieve __ that you are __

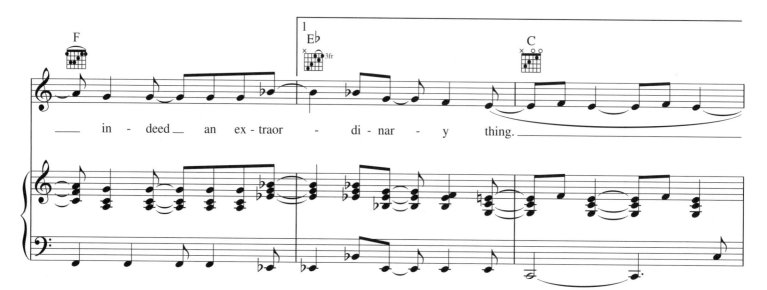

__ in - deed __ an ex - traor - di - nar - y thing. __

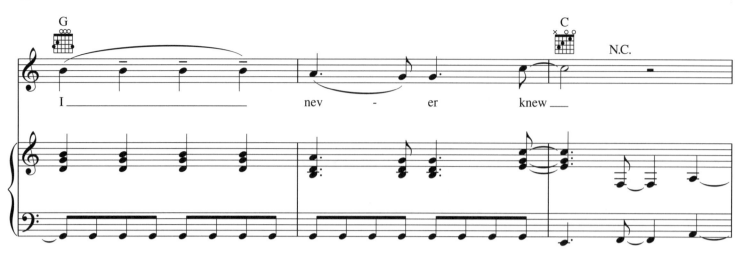

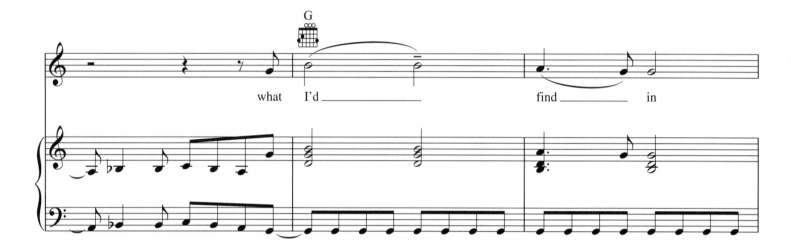

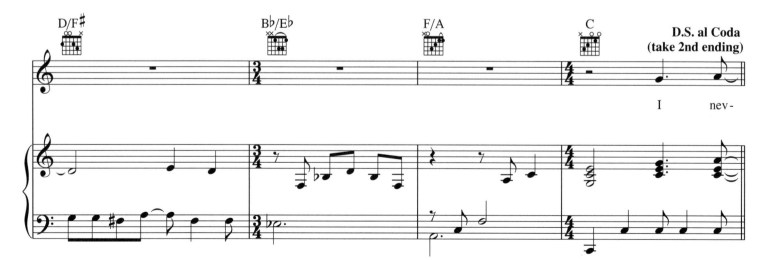

CODA

I do ___ be - lieve ___ that you are ___

___ in - deed ___ an ex - traor - di - nar - y thing. ___

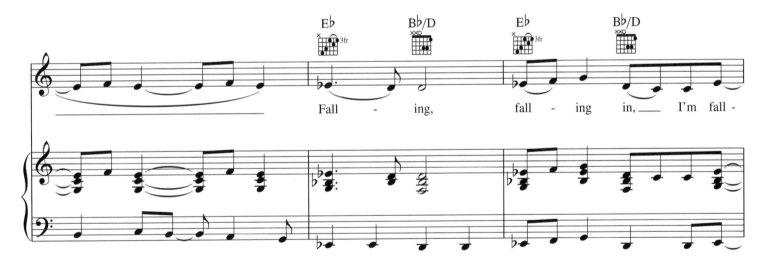

___ Fall - ing, fall - ing in, ___ I'm fall -

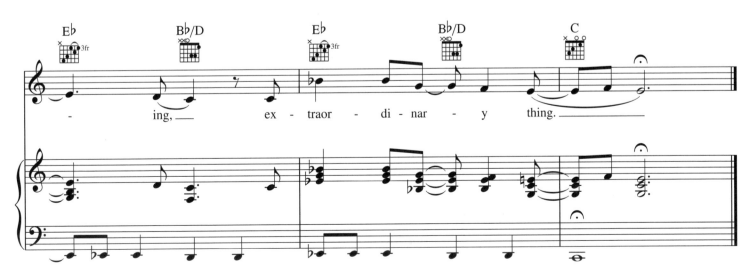

- ing, ___ ex - traor - di - nar - y thing. ___

I DREAM OF SPRING

Words and Music by k.d. lang
and DAVID PILTCH

With yearning

She ___ ar - rives ___ like

au - tumn in a rain - storm, ___ threat of thun - der ___ a -

bove. I'll re - turn ___ from the

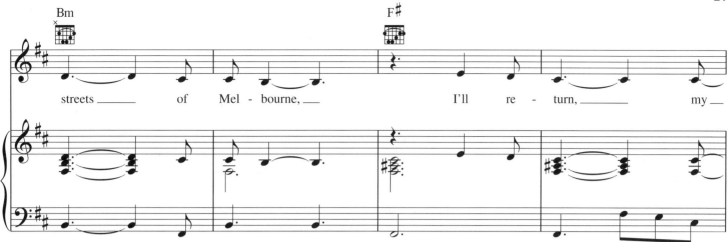

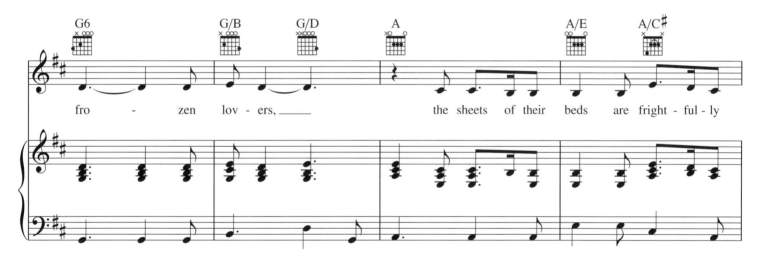

To Coda

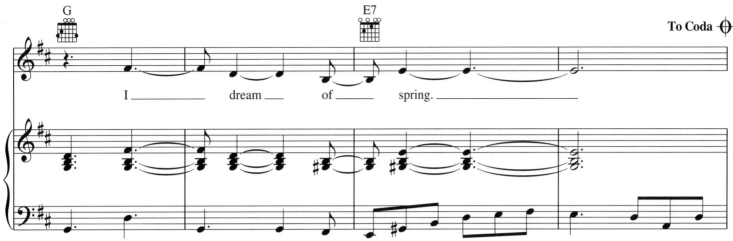

I _____ dream ___ of _____ spring. _____

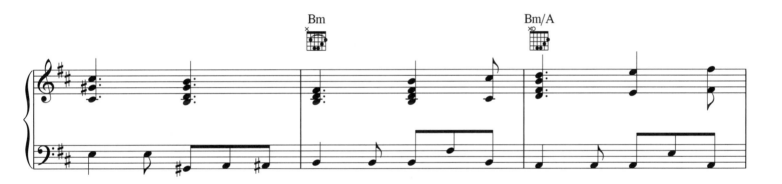

D.S. al Coda

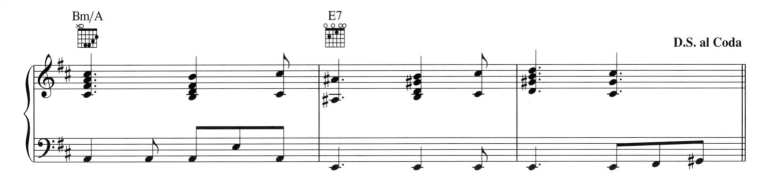

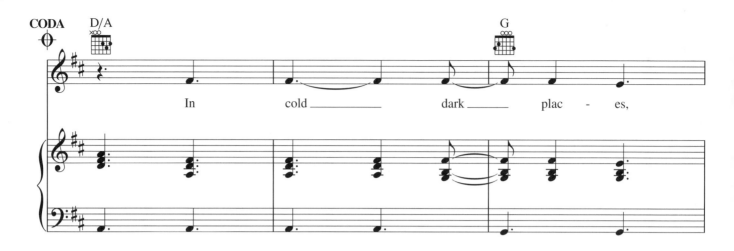

In cold _____ dark _____ plac - es,

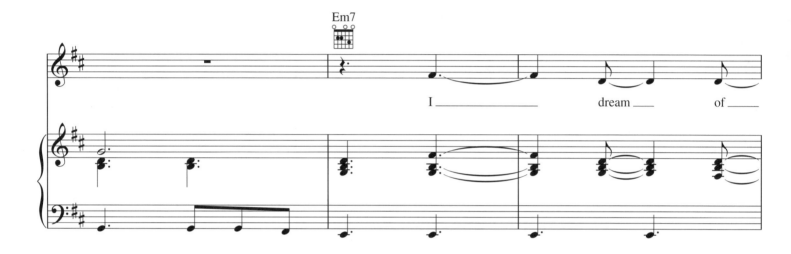

I _____ dream _____ of _____

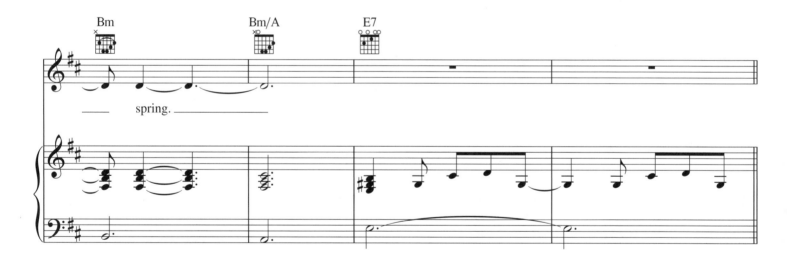

_____ spring. _____

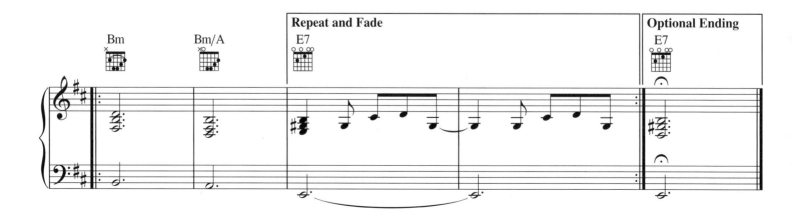

SUMMERFLING

Words and Music by k.d. lang
and DAVID PILTCH

Moderately fast

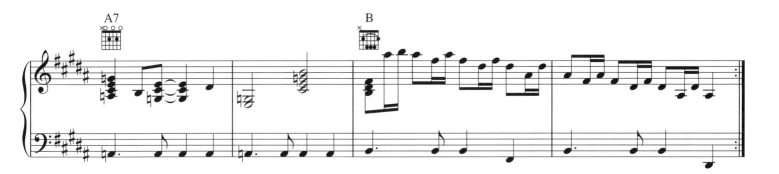

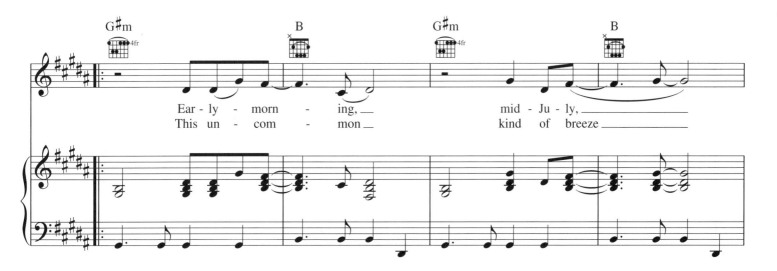

Ear - ly - morn - ing, ___ mid - Ju - ly, ___
This un - com - mon ___ kind of breeze ___

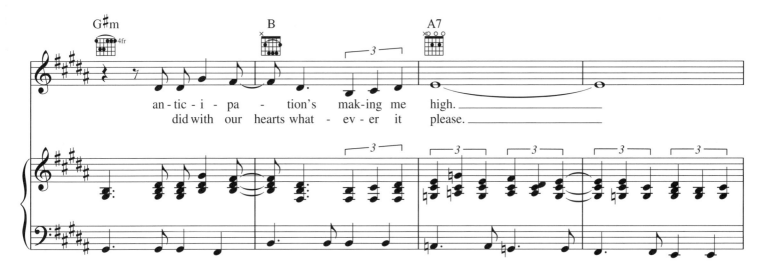

an - tic - i - pa - tion's mak - ing me high. ___
did with our hearts what - ev - er it please. ___

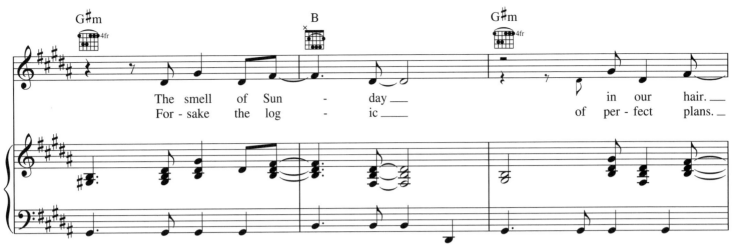

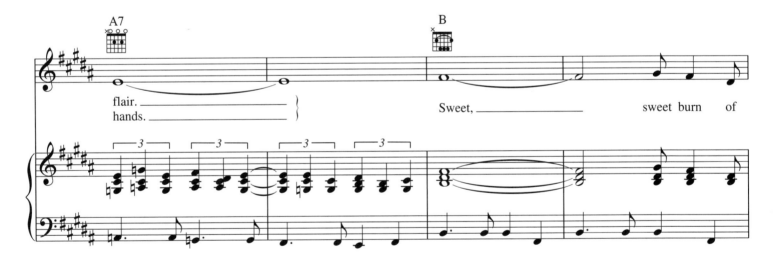

my sum - mer - fling.

Laugh, _____ oh, _____ how we ____ would laugh at an - y - thing ____

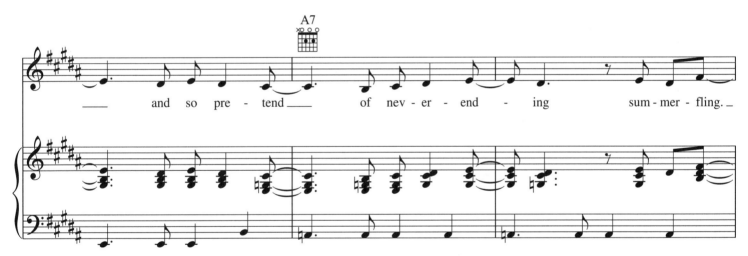

____ and so pre - tend ____ of nev - er - end - ing sum - mer - fling. ____

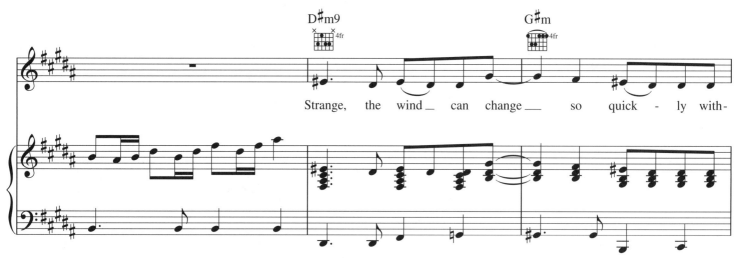

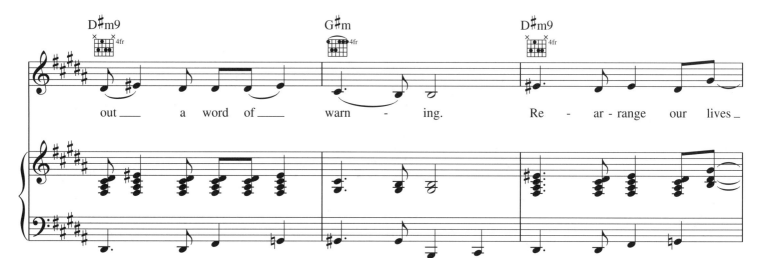

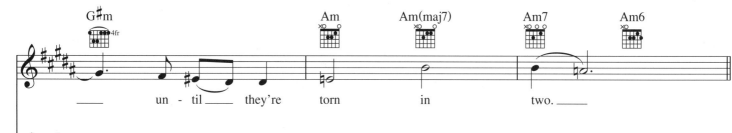

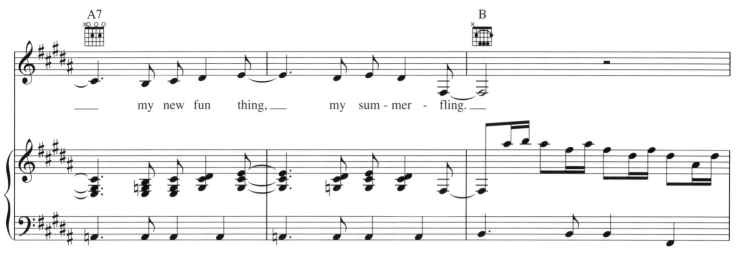

my new fun thing, ___ my sum-mer - fling. ___

Laugh, ___ oh, ___ how we ___ would

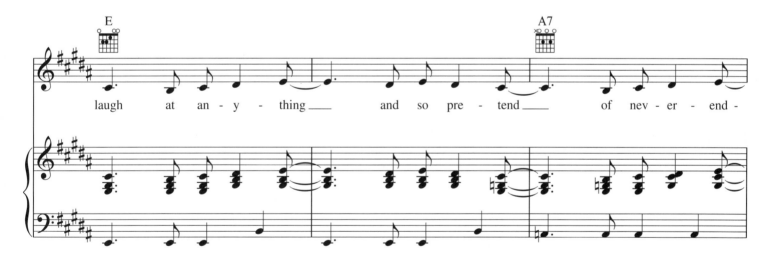

laugh at an-y - thing ___ and so pre-tend ___ of nev-er - end-

Repeat ad lib. and Fade

-ing sum-mer - fling. ___

THE MIND OF LOVE

Words and Music by k.d. lang
and BEN MINK

Gently, in moderate tempo

Talk-ing _____ to my-self here _____ is caus-ing

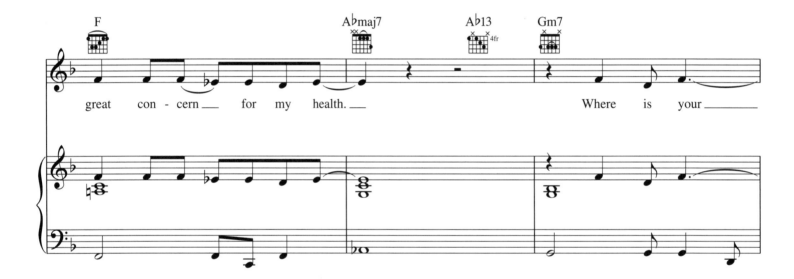

great con-cern _____ for my health. _____ Where is your _____

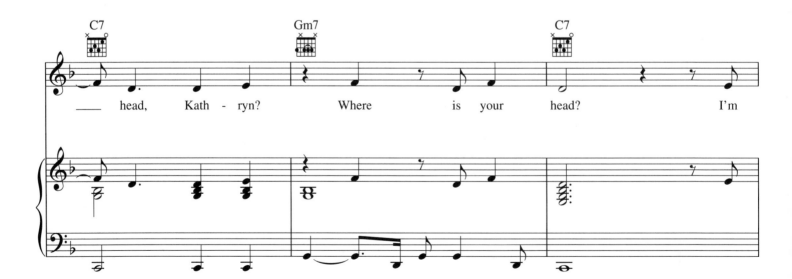

_____ head, Kath-ryn? Where is your head? I'm

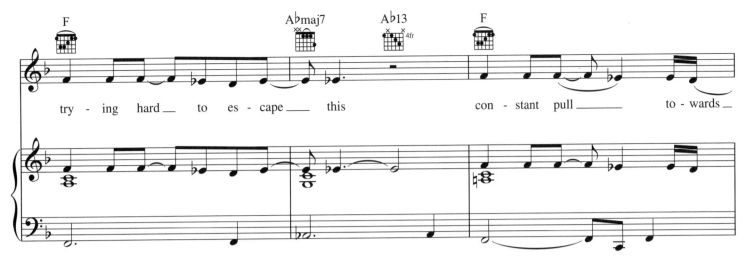

try - ing hard __ to es - cape __ this con - stant pull __ to - wards __

__ ache. __ Why __ do you fight, Kath - ryn?

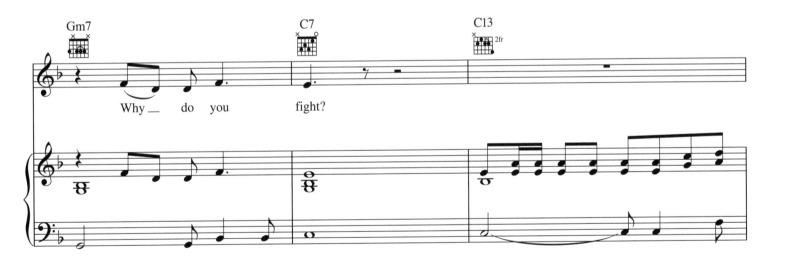

Why __ do you fight?

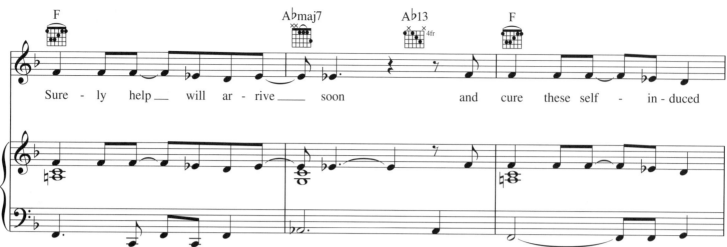

Sure - ly help __ will ar - rive __ soon and cure these self - in - duced

wounds. Why hurt your - self, __ Kath - ryn?

Why hurt your - self? __ Why hurt your -

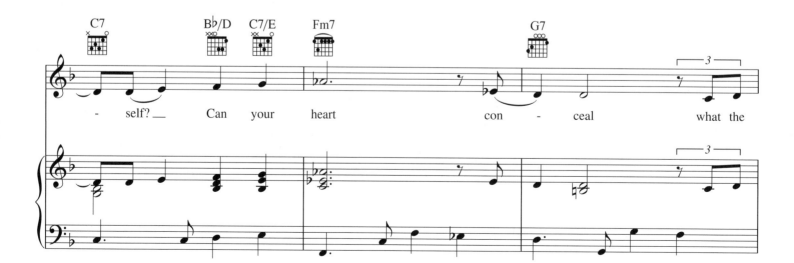

- self? __ Can your heart con - ceal what the

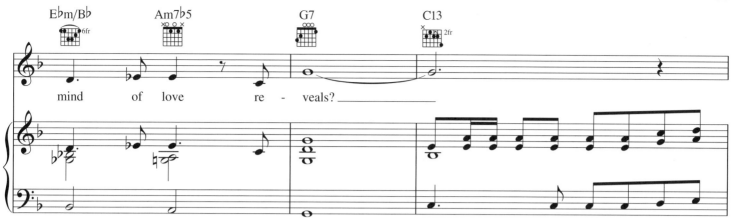

mind of love re - veals? _____

I'm talk - ing ___ to my - self ___ a - gain. It's caus - ing

great con - cern ___ for ___ my health. Where ___ is your head, _

Kath - ryn? Where __ is your head? __

Where _ is your _____ head, ____ Kath - ryn? Where _ is your ____

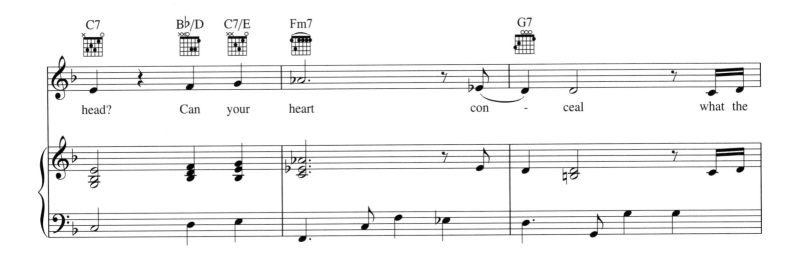

head? Can your heart con - ceal what the

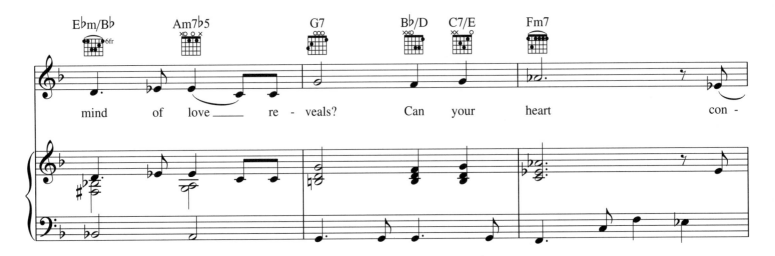

mind of love ____ re - veals? Can your heart con -

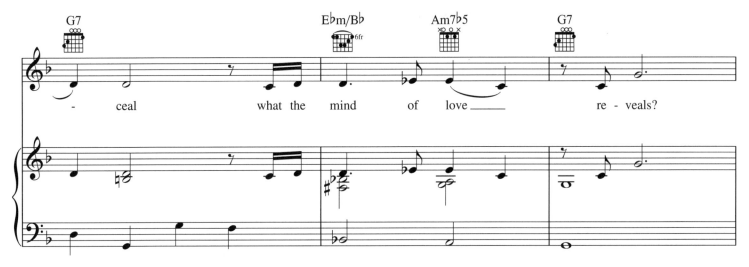

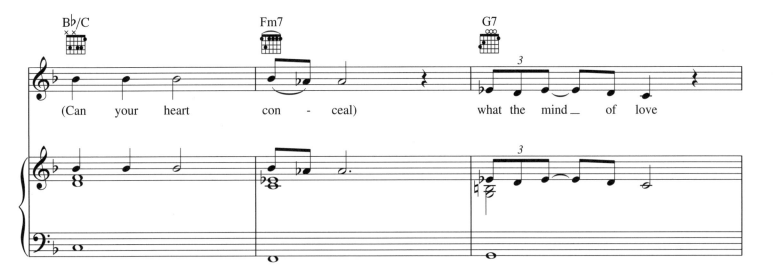

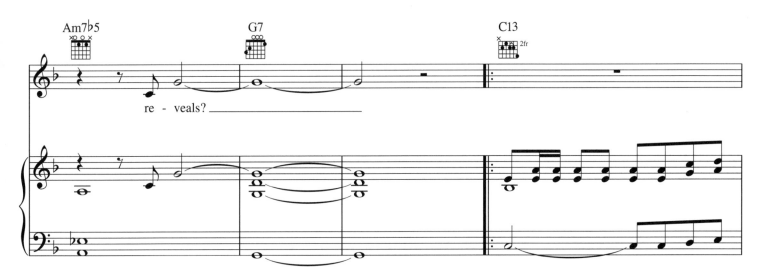

MISS CHATELAINE

Words and Music by k.d. lang
and BEN MINK

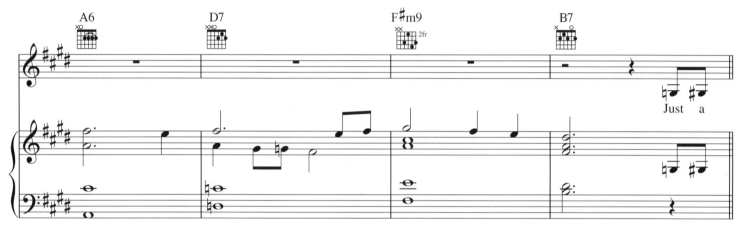

come   Miss   Chat - e - laine.   Just a
come   Miss   Chat - e -   laine.
come   Miss   Chat - e -   laine.

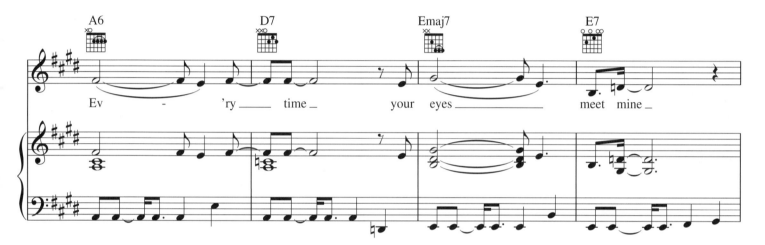

Ev - 'ry _____ time _   your   eyes _____ meet mine _

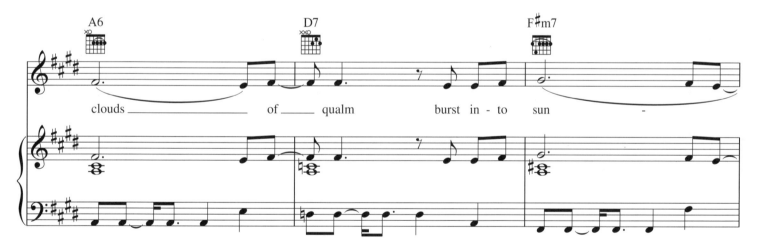

clouds _____ of ____ qualm   burst in - to   sun -

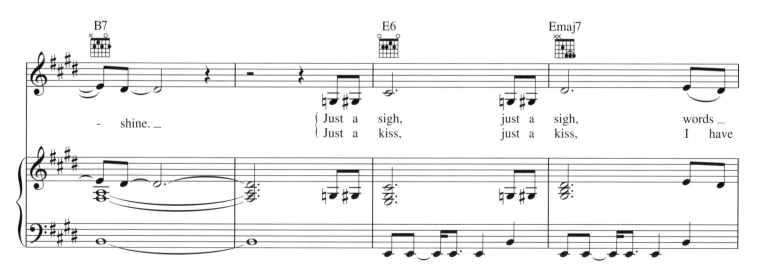

- shine. _   Just a   sigh,   just a   sigh,   words _
               Just a   kiss,   just a   kiss,   I have

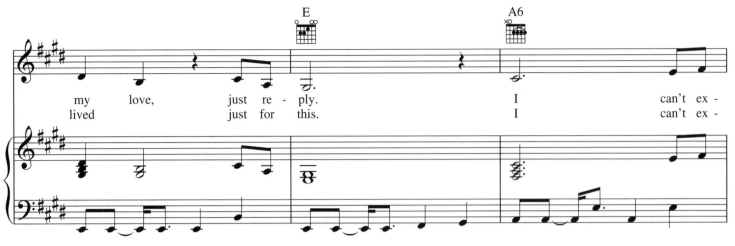

my love, just re - ply.   I   can't ex -
lived just for this.   I   can't ex -

To Coda ⊕

plain why I've be - come   Miss   Chat - e -
plain why I've be - come   Miss   Chat - e -

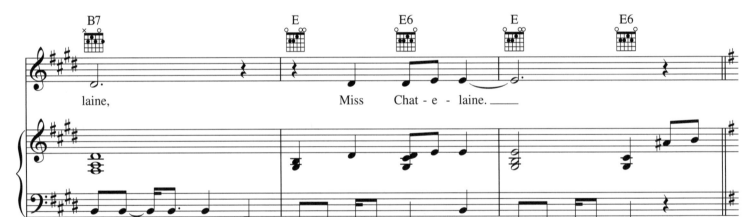

laine,   Miss Chat - e - laine. ___

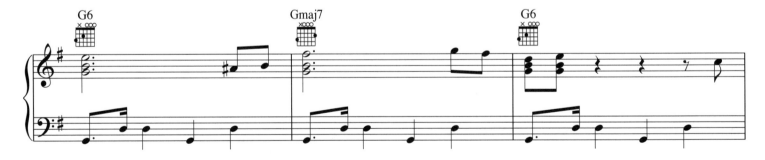

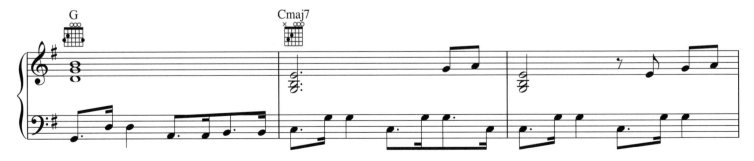

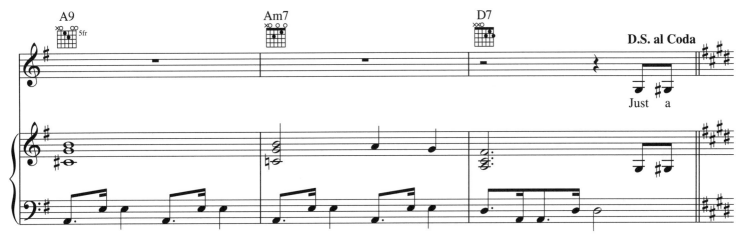

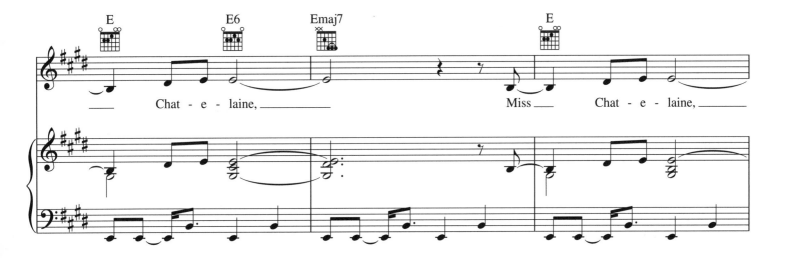

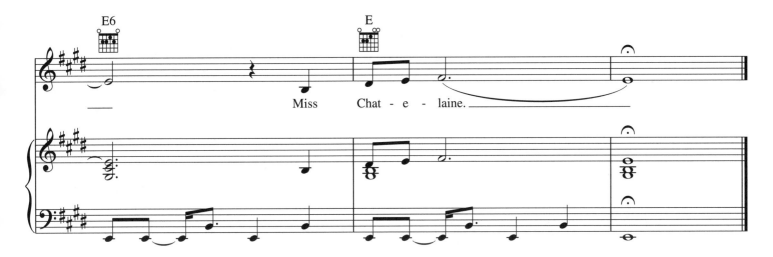

NOWHERE TO STAND

Words and Music by
k.d. lang

As things start _____ to ___ sur - face _____
ta - bles _____ have turned now _____
mem - 'ries _____ of chil - dren _____

and tears _____ come on _____ down.
with a child _____ of her _____ own.
are writ - ten in _____ stone, _____

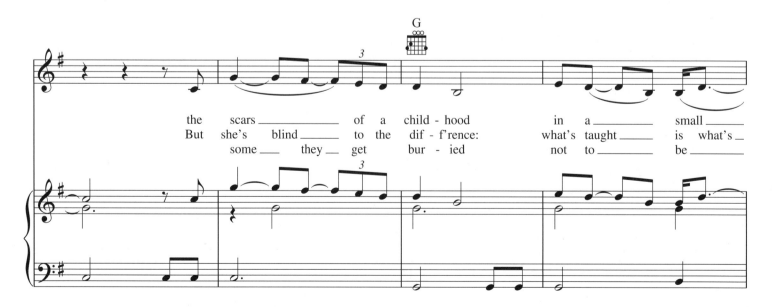

the scars _____ of a child - hood in a _____ small _____
But she's blind _____ to the dif - f'rence: what's taught _____ is what's ___
some ___ they ___ get bur - ied not to _____ be

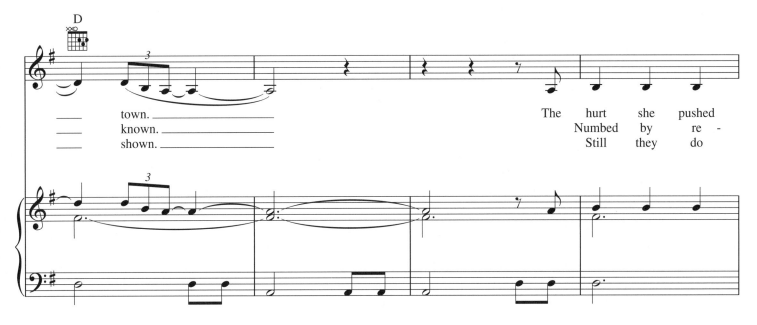

town. _____ The hurt she pushed
known. _____ Numbed by re -
shown. _____ Still they do

in - ward _____ is start - ing _____
ac - tion _____ and stripped of _____
lin - ger _____ deep down _____

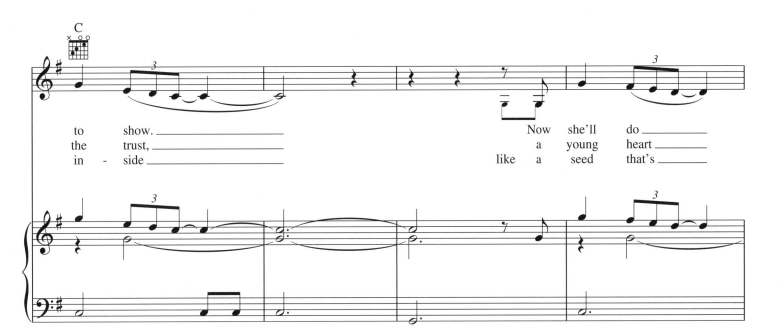

to show. _____ Now she'll do _____
the trust, _____ a young heart _____
in - side _____ like a seed that's _____

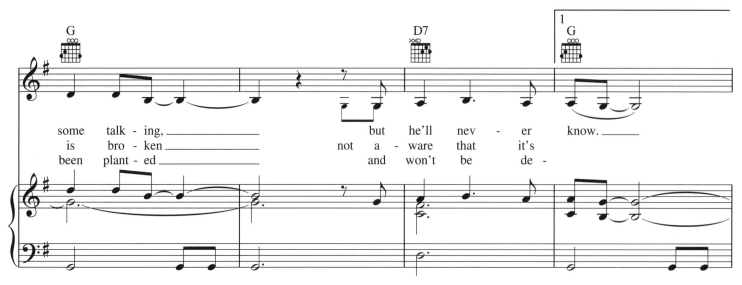

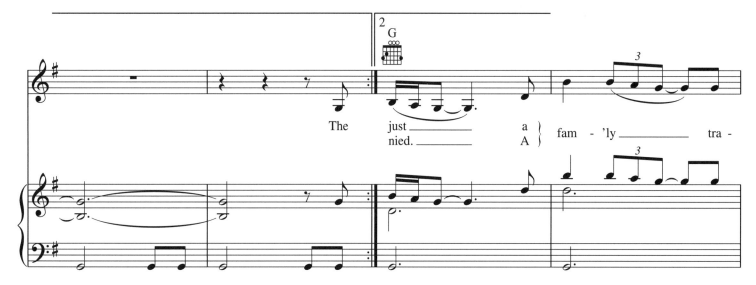

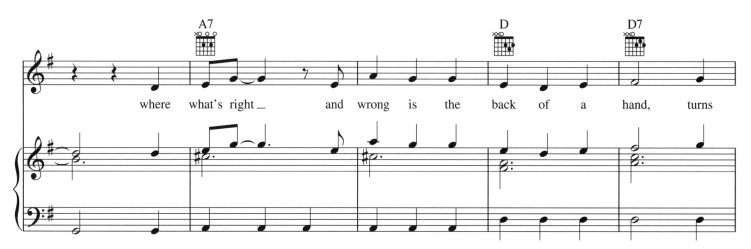

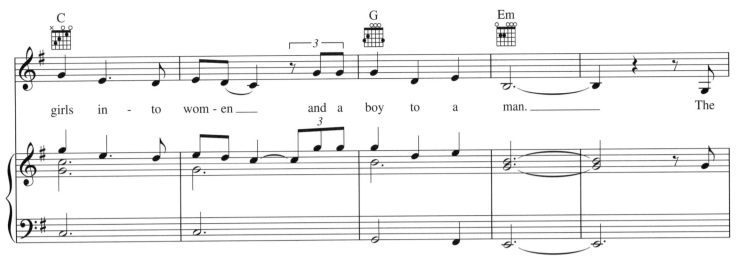

girls in - to wom - en ____ and a boy to a man. ____ The

rights of the chil - dren ____ have no - where to stand,

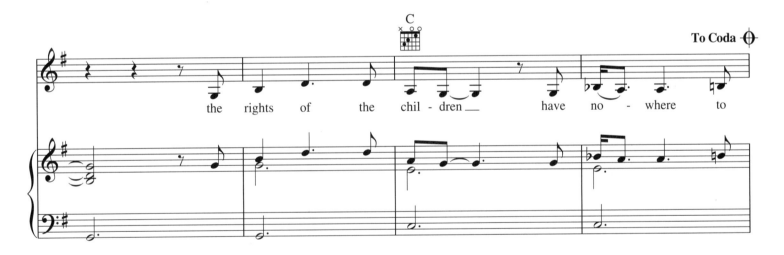

the rights of the chil - dren ____ have no - where to

To Coda ⊕

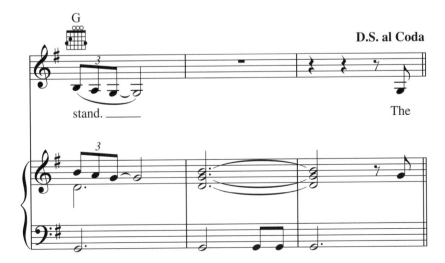

stand. ____ The

D.S. al Coda

CODA ⊕

stand. ____

rall.

PULLIN' BACK THE REINS

Words and Music by k.d. lang
and BEN MINK

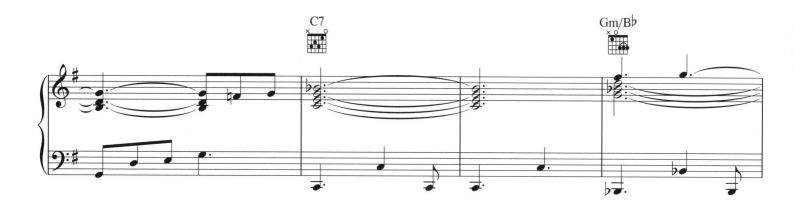

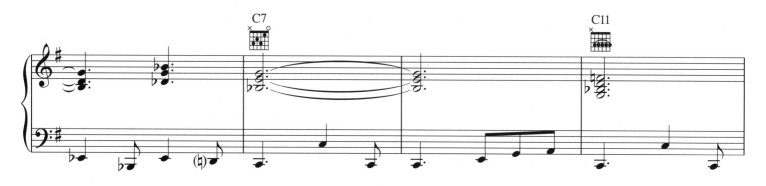

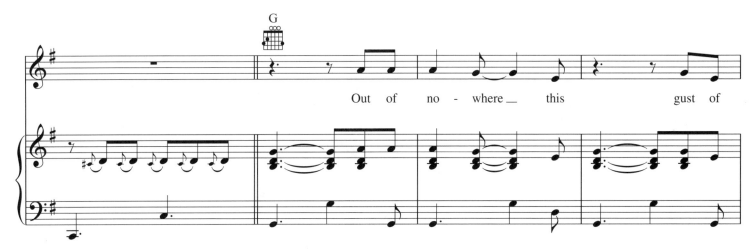

Out of no-where ___ this ___ gust of

wind ___ brushed ___ my hair ___ and kissed ___ my ___

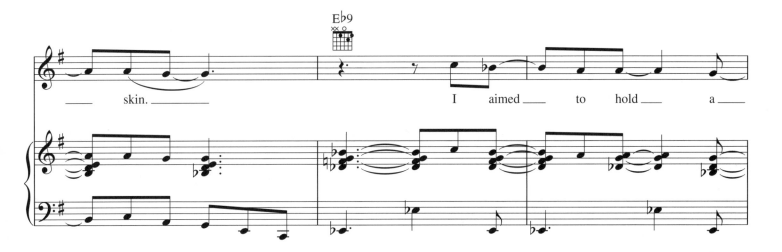

___ skin. ___ I aimed ___ to hold ___ a ___

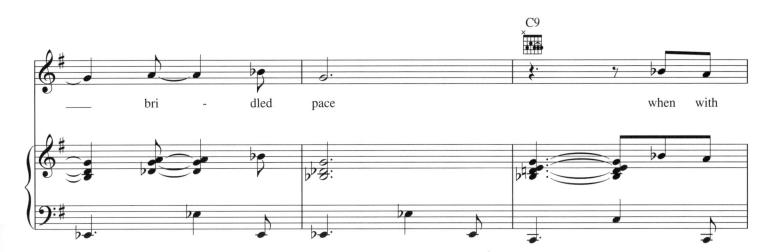

___ bri - dled pace when with

love it - self ___ I came face to face. _____ Pull - ing

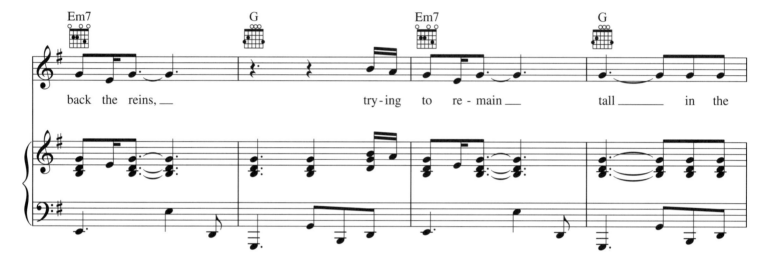

back the reins, ___ try - ing to re - main ___ tall _____ in the

sad - dle ___ when all _____ that we had, well, ran a -

way with a will of its own. _____

I know your soul ___ is ___ wild and free, _____ like ___

___ this gal - lop - ing in - side ___ me. ___ Tossed ___

by in - stinct and where ___ we land is

D.S. al Coda

vast and cer - tain of all _____ that's ___ planned. _____

48

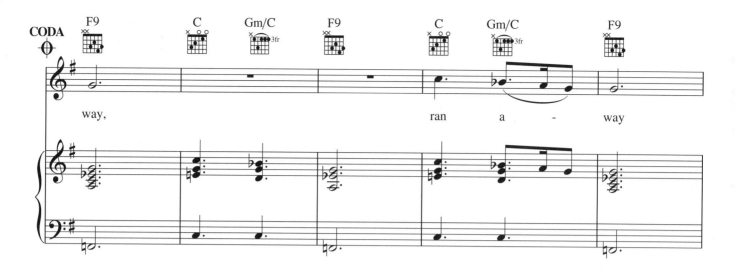

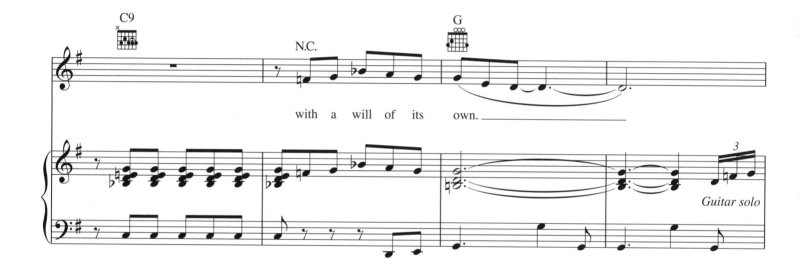

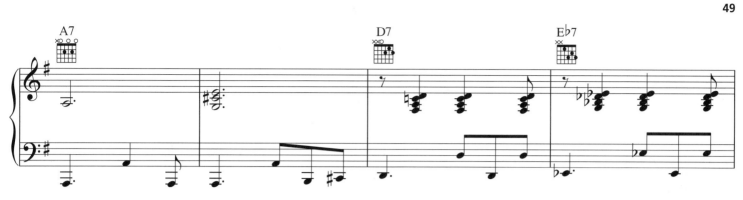

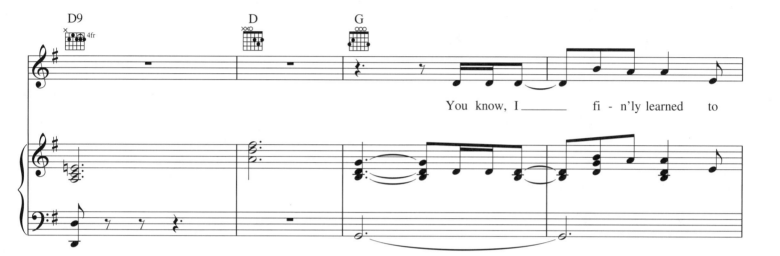

You know, I _____ fi - n'ly learned to

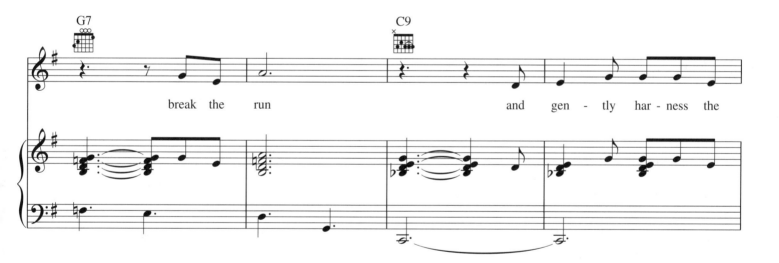

break the run   and gen - tly har - ness the

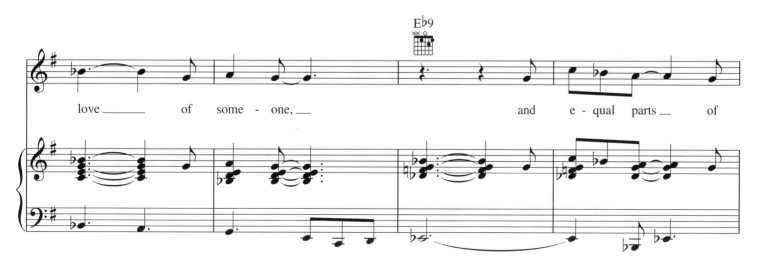

love _____ of some - one, ___   and e - qual parts ___ of

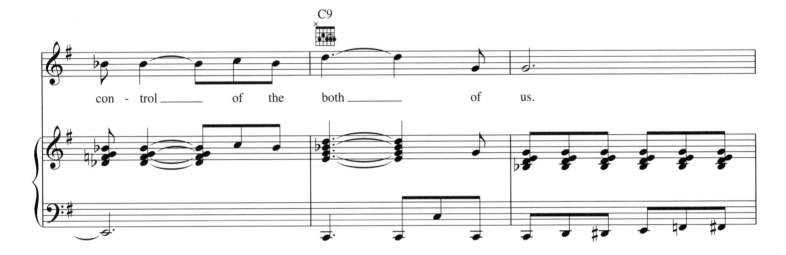

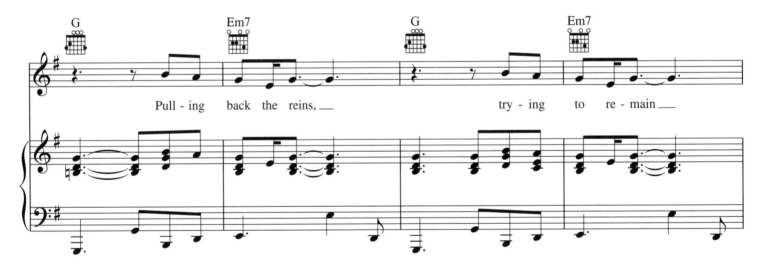

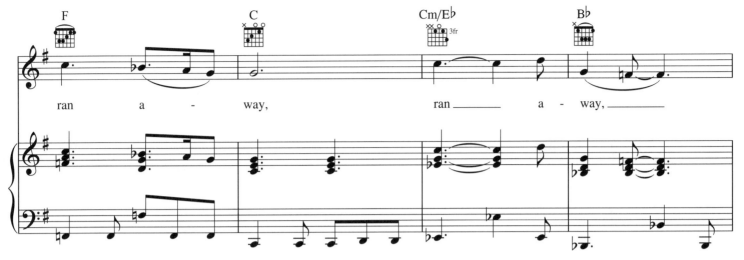

ran a - way, ran a - way,

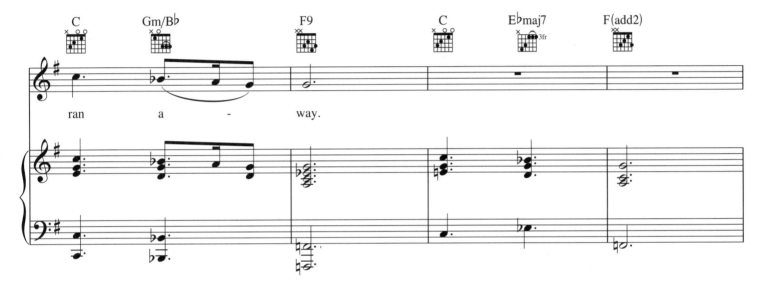

ran a - way.

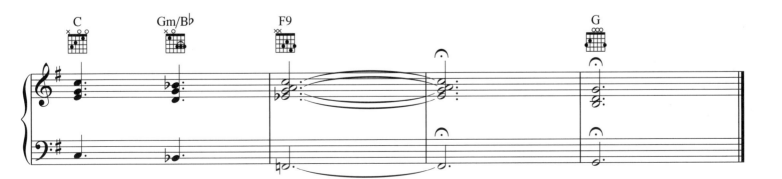

SIMPLE

Words and Music by k.d. lang
and DAVID PILTCH

Flaw-less light __ in a dark - en ing air, a - lone and shin-ing __ there.

Love will not e - lude you, love is sim -

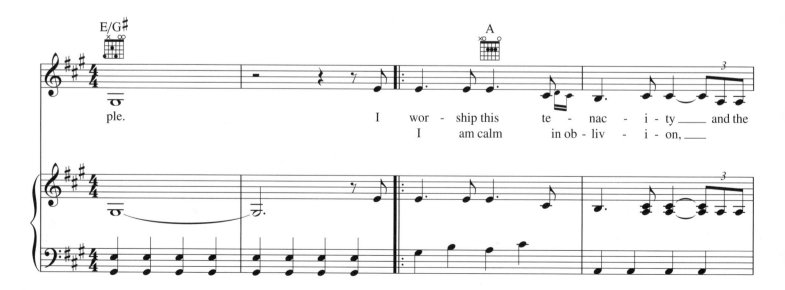

ple.

I wor - ship this te - nac-i - ty __ and the
I am calm in ob - liv - i - on, __

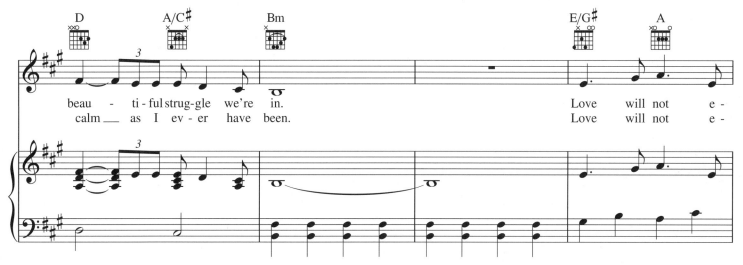

beau - ti-ful strug-gle we're in. Love will not e -
calm___ as I ev-er have been. Love will not e -

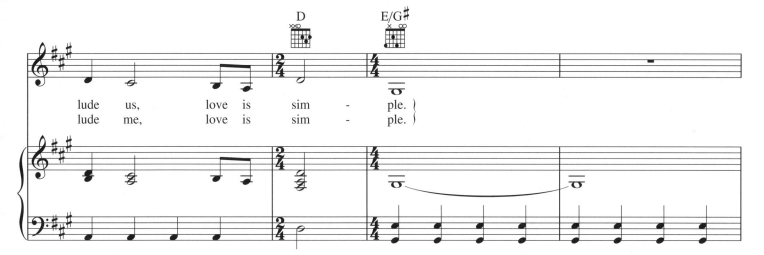

lude us, love is sim - ple. }
lude me, love is sim - ple. }

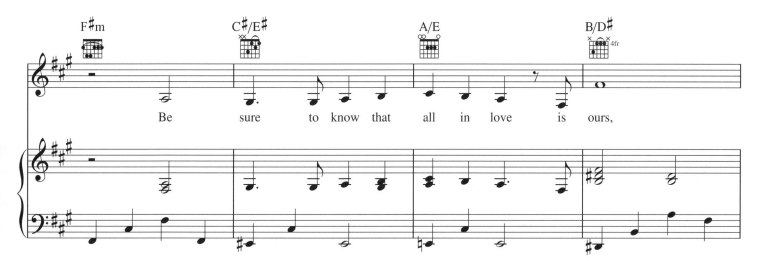

Be sure to know that all in love is ours,

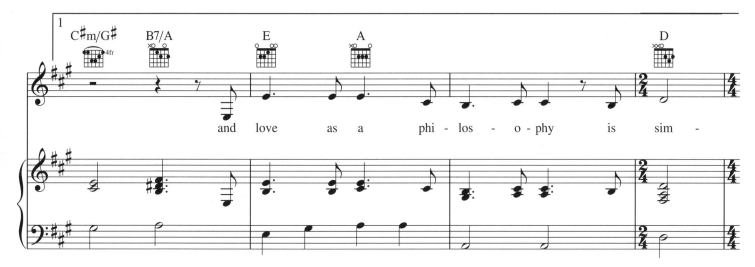

and love as a phi - los - o - phy is sim -

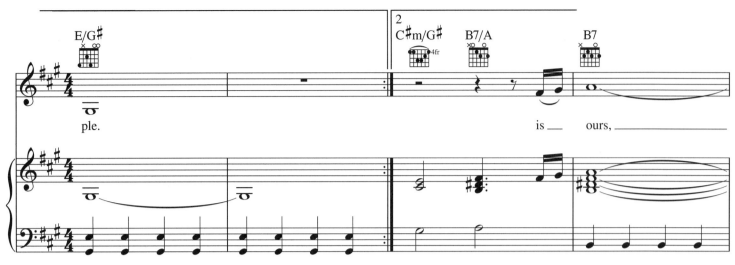

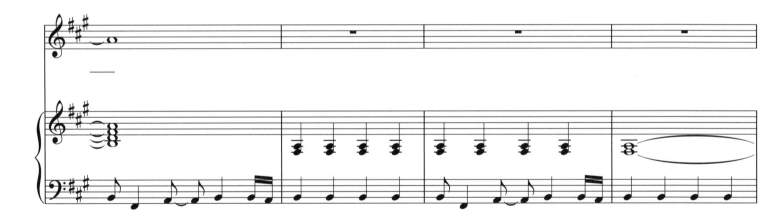

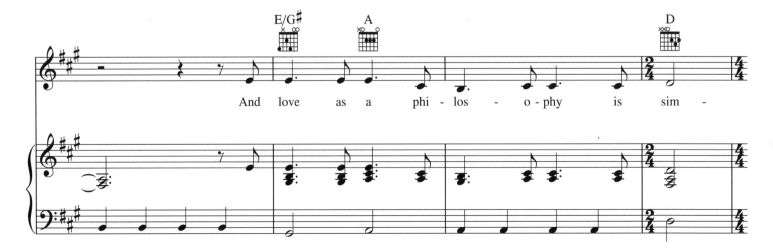

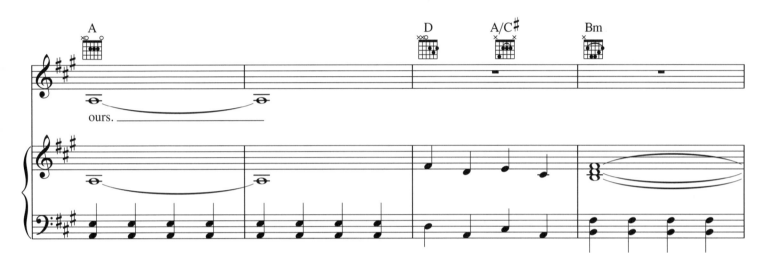

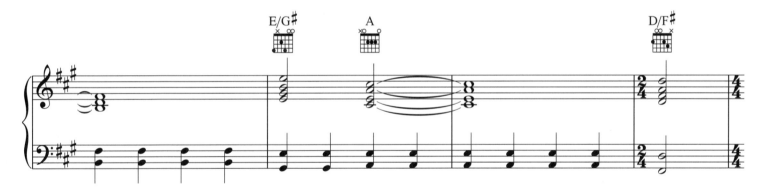

THREAD

Words and Music by k.d. lang
and DAVID PILTCH

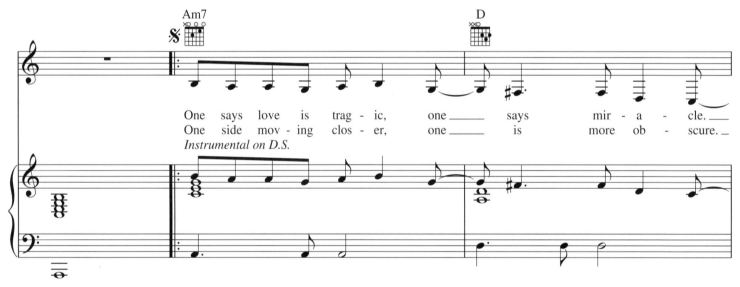

One says love is trag - ic, one ____ says mir - a - cle. ____
One side mov - ing clos - er, one ____ is more ob - scure. ____

Instrumental on D.S.

One be - comes a scep - tic, one __
One side feel - ing o - pen, one __

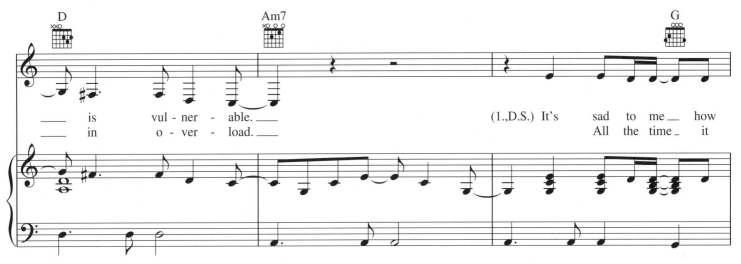

is vul - ner - a - ble. ___ (1.,D.S.) It's sad to me ___ how
in o - ver - load. ___ All the time ___ it

quick - ly we de - fine ___ what is wrong ___ with
takes to build things up, ___ in no time ___ fly ___

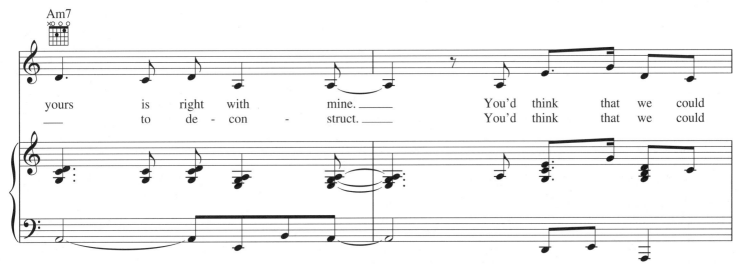

yours is right with mine. ___ You'd think that we could
___ to de - con - struct. ___ You'd think that we could

To Coda

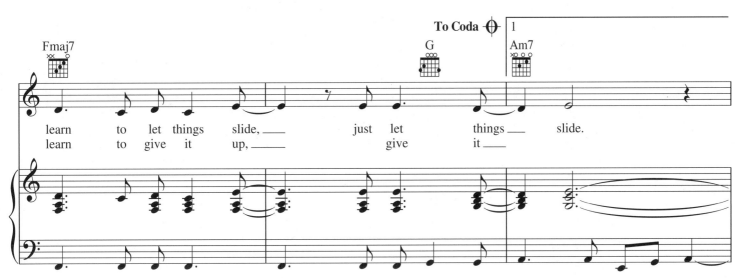

learn to let things slide, ___ just let things ___ slide.
learn to give it up, ___ let give it ___

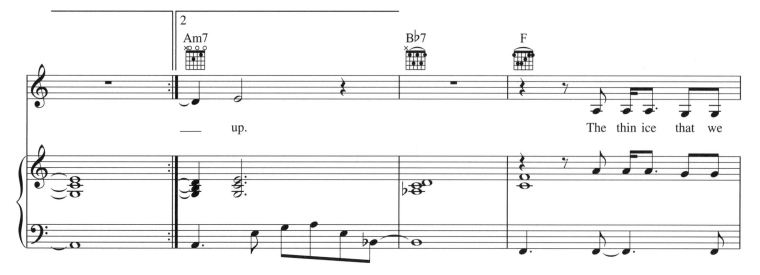

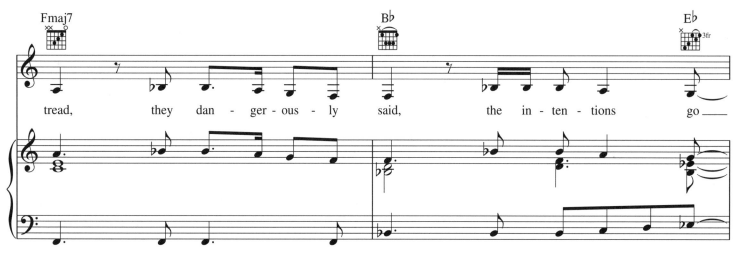

I'm caught up in ___ the back ___ and forth ___ of

bal - anc - ing ___ my ___ fear. ___ I'll tell you, though, ___ for

what it's worth, ___ I fell ___ for you, my dear. ___

D.S. al Coda

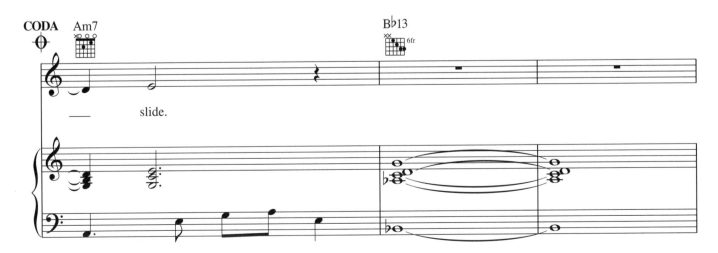

___ slide.

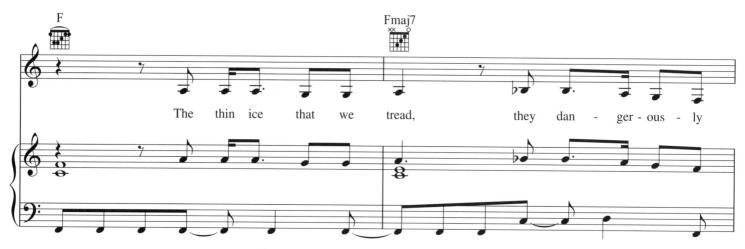

The thin ice that we tread, they dan - ger - ous - ly

said, the in - ten - tions go _____ fall - ing through. _ And _ you, _

_ I had you in _ my web, _ now here I am

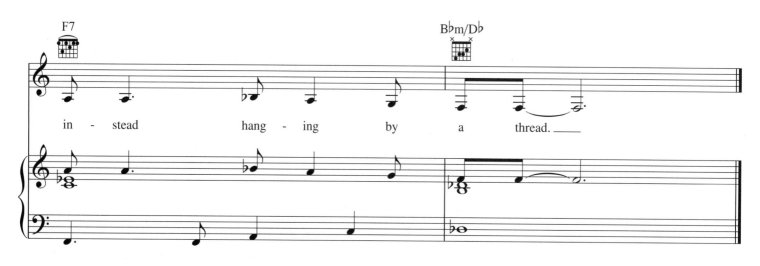

in - stead hang - ing by a thread. _____

WASH ME CLEAN

Words and Music by
k.d. lang

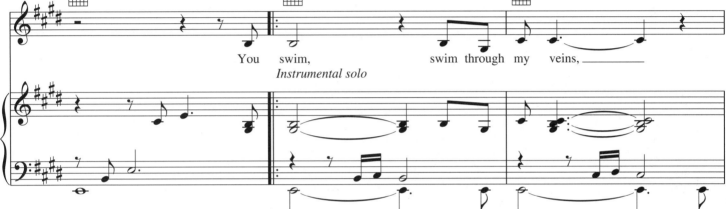

You swim, swim through my veins, _____
Instrumental solo

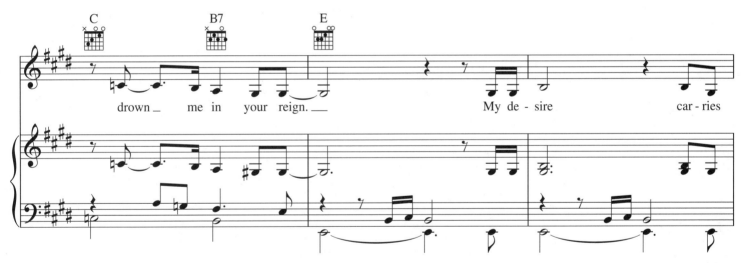

drown _ me in your reign. _ My de- sire car- ries

no shame. My _ will will har- bor no _ pain.
Solo ends

quench _____ love's _ dry - ing well. Wash, _____ wash me

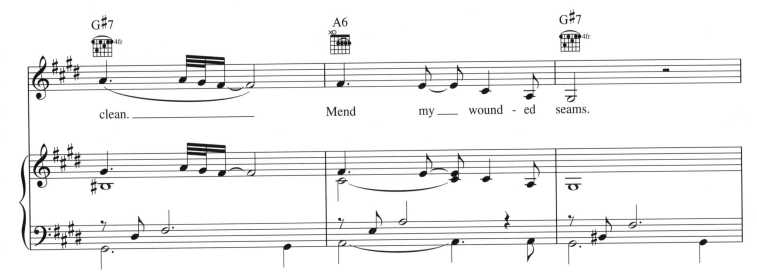

clean. _____ Mend my ___ wound - ed seams.

Cleanse my _____ tar - nished dreams.

TRAIL OF BROKEN HEARTS

Words and Music by k.d. lang
and BEN MINK

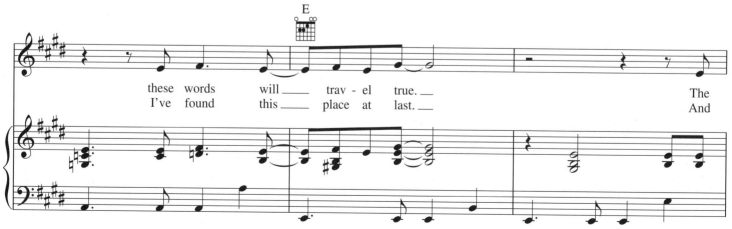

god - speed _ of trust _____ will _____ set - tle _____ the dust _
here will _____ re - main _____ with _____ on - ly _____ the aim _

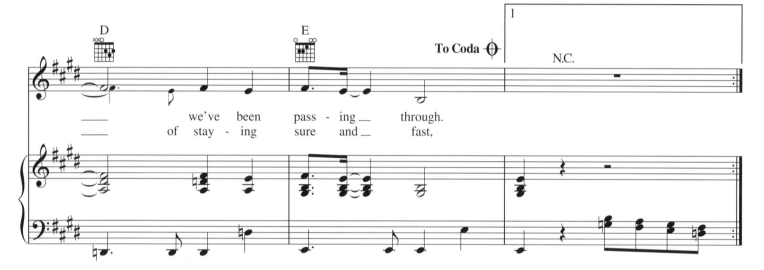

_____ we've been pass - ing ___ through.
_____ of stay - ing sure and ___ fast,

leav - ing just a part _____ down the trail _____

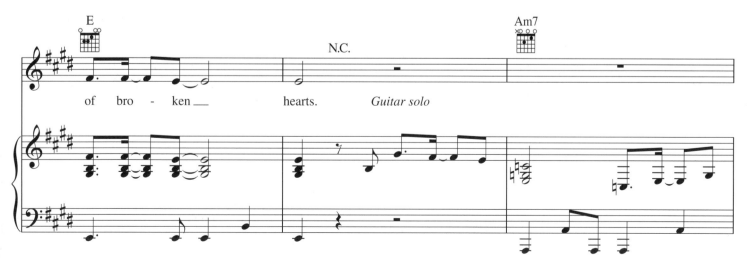

of bro - ken ___ hearts. *Guitar solo*

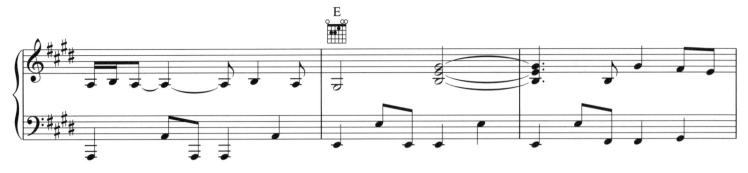

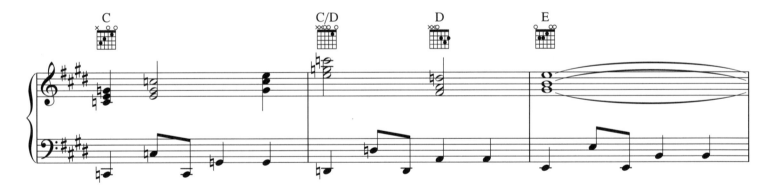

D.S. al Coda
(take 1st verse)

Solo ends   Trail   of

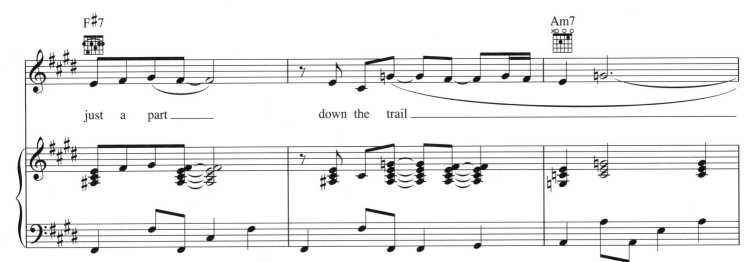

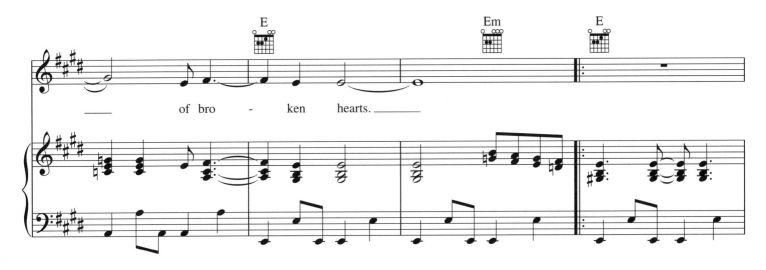

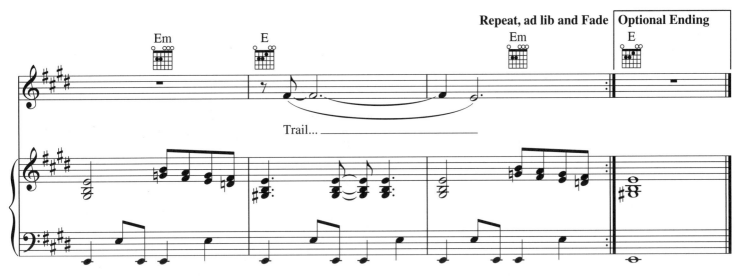

YOU'RE OK

Words and Music by k.d. lang
and BEN MINK

could it be ___ that I ___ an - noy ___ you, flaunt - ing ways ___ that I ___
Can you of - fer some ___ as - sist - ance, let me in ___ on how, ___

___ a - dore ___ you. I have no con - trol ___ here ei - ther ___
___ for in - stance, I should be con - vinc - ing you to ___

___ way. }
___ sway. }
I ___ a -

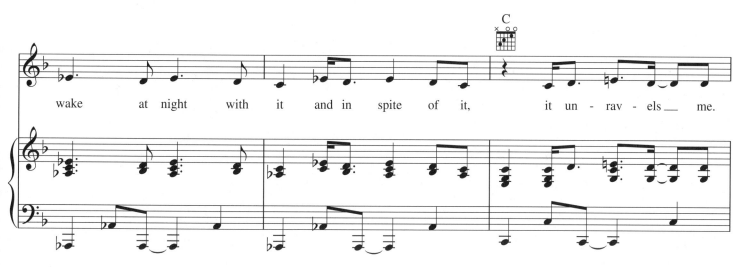

wake at night with it and in spite of it, it un - rav - els ___ me.

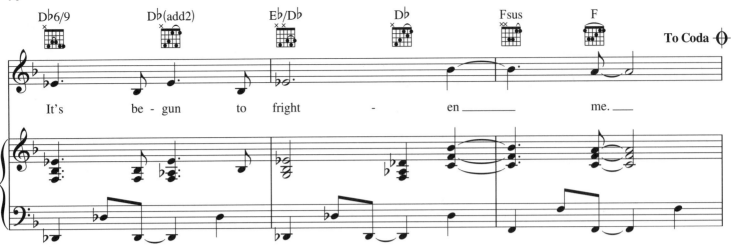

It's be-gun to fright - en _____ me. _____

Is it so _____ that my _____ per - sist - ence

blocks the path _____ of least _____ re - sist - ance. May - be I'm just

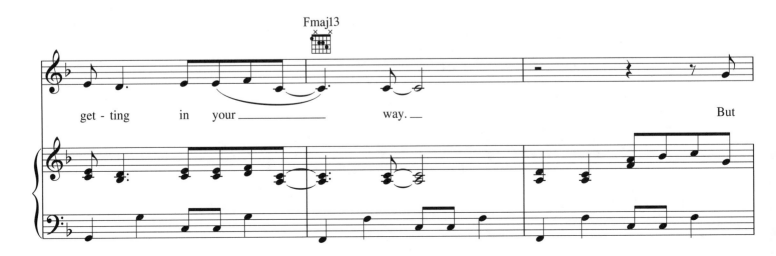

get - ting in your _____ way. _____ But

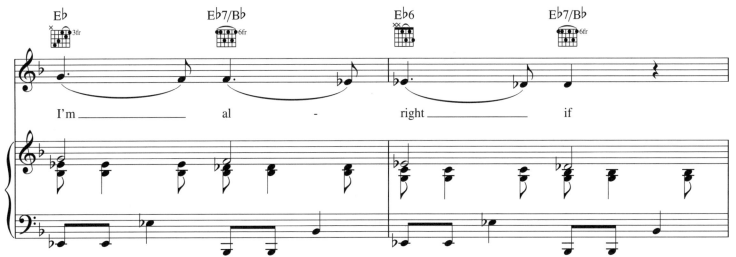

I'm _____ al - right _____ if

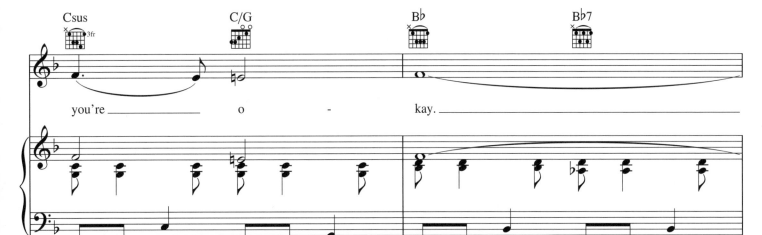

you're _____ o - kay. _____

_____ I'm _____ al - right _____ if

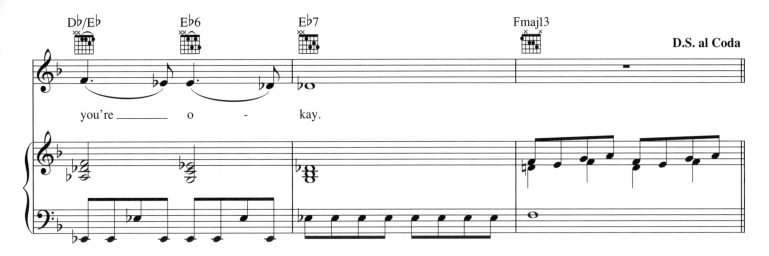

you're _____ o - kay.

D.S. al Coda

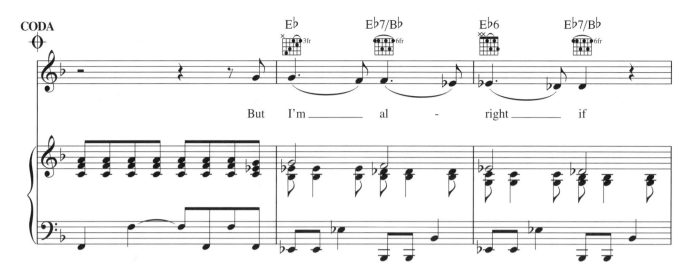

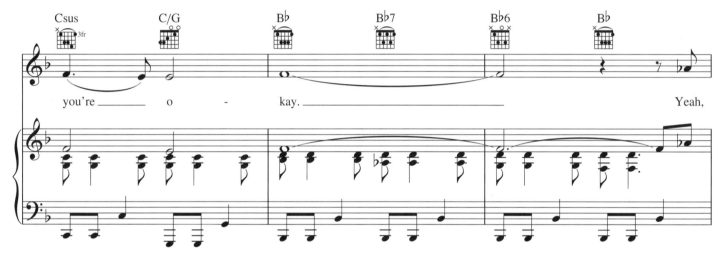

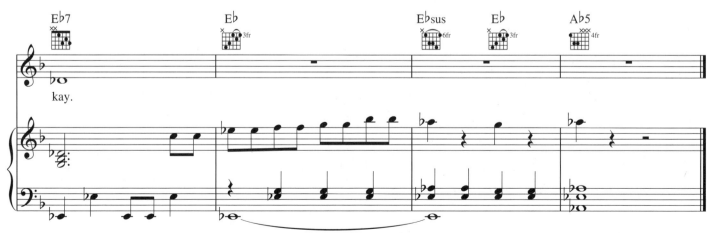